CROSSING THE RUBICON

WISDOM TRAILS WITH THE OLD MONK

KRISHNA KUMAR MARAYIL

This is a masterpiece of a book - short and concise, yet extremely eloquently presented by Krishna Kumar. An Executive Coach of international standing for many decades, Kumar has distilled the core learnings from his experience and practice in this book. The poems at the end of each chapter present a welcome break and help to clarify the subtle nuances. As one goes through the book, one cannot help but feel the cathartic process set in motion inside the mind to free it from hubris and the chaotic noise of daily existence. A superlative effort by any standards!

Subir Chakraborty, Ex MD & CEO, Exide Industries Ltd, Independent Director, Business Mentor, Kolkata (India)

People of all ages occasionally find themselves seeking meaning in life or work or relationships, and many often seek the help of others to resolve their dilemma. Crossing the Rubicon is a beautifully written book that is fun to read and very engaging. Presented as a conversation between a Seeker and an Old Monk, it has two simple messages. The first, indulge in self-reflection – look inwards – to find meaning. The second, if others seek your help, rather than thrust your considered view on the seekers guide them to self-reflection – they will find the answers themselves."

Abhoy K Ojha, Ph D, Professor, Indian Institute of Management, Bengaluru (India)

"Crossing the Rubicon" is a profound exploration of leadership and self-discovery, seamlessly blending timeless wisdom with contemporary insights. Krishna Kumar skillfully guides readers through the journey of resilient leadership, embracing vulnerability and the fear of failure as catalysts for growth. The narrative, led by the enigmatic Old Monk, delves into themes of authentic leadership, the power of silence and leader as a mentor. It encourages readers to awaken their inner voices and develop a deep sense of self-awareness through introspection. With beautiful poetry and insightful questions and anecdotes, Krishna Kumar has crafted a work that is both inspiring and practical, providing valuable insights for those seeking to lead with both heart and mind. "Crossing the Rubicon" is a treasure trove of wisdom for anyone ready to embark on a transformative journey."

Sheenam Ohrie, Managing Director, Broadridge Financial Solutions, India (Bengaluru)

A beautifully written and thought-provoking story highlighting the value and beauty of living in the present moment with the gentle but clear nudge towards self-discovery. The Old Monk's tales will make an immediate and positive impact to your personal growth and stay with you long after you turn the final page.

Craig Thielen - Chief Innovation Officer, Trissential, Minnesota (USA)

What a journey this book takes you on! At first glance, it seems to be a conversation between the Monk and the Chief, but as I read, I realized it was much more — a mirror reflecting our own doubts and questions about the realities we navigate. Deep down, aren't we all both the Monk and the Chief, caught at the crossroads of wisdom and ambition, stillness and action?

The tension between these opposing forces shapes not only our destinies but also the essence of who we are. To walk this delicate tightrope of balance is no small feat, and in this endeavor, we could hardly ask for a better guide than Krishna Kumar. Knowing the author of this spiritual odyssey personally is a privilege I treasure. It's not just his wisdom that brings joy into my life but the sheer energy of his presence, which feels like an otherworldly gift of mental strength. Thank you, Krishna, for penning this profound work that holds the potential to be a personal revelation for every reader.

Zsadany Vecsey, Founder and CEO at ALEAS Simulations, Inc. Budapest (a business co-created by Prof. Mihaly Csikszentmihalyi)

Crossing the Rubicon" is a delightful little book written in the traditional format of the 'Champu' with a classic theme. The serene and omniscient Old Master guiding the eager young pupil. The real teacher does not instruct. He gently guides his charges and gives them insights that help them arrive at a solution. The book leaves one wanting more.

Dr T M Kasturirangan, Financial Consultant, Chennai (India)

Is it fate, karma, or mere coincidence that leads us to the wisdom we most need?

Many moons ago, I was introduced to the wisdom of the Old Monk and soon found myself fully engaged with its depth —long before these stories found their home between the covers of a book. I stopped wondering. The real question became: How deeply can wisdom shape a soul?

In "Crossing the Rubicon", the story unfolds within you, inviting a quiet dialogue with yourself. The Old Monk comes alive through a masterfully woven narrative, each word tapping into the core of one's being. Like ripples in water, his wisdom lingers, stretching beyond the chapters, awakening forgotten strengths and igniting a chain reaction of introspection and growth. But here's the true genius—the Old Monk never points to a path. He nudges. He hints. He lets you find your own way. And in doing so, he leaves behind a wisdom that echoes long after the final page.

The question now is: Where will you go from here?

Bibi Ohlsson, Thinking partner, Strengths based Self-Leadership Coach, Bergen, Norway

To paraphrase from one of the deft touches in *Crossing the Rubicon*, Krishna Kumar has "used a path that isn't used regularly". He has smoothly interwoven pithy worldly wisdom from the Old Monk with epiphanies that the Chief discovers into a compelling story. That story captures much of the author's professional experience as a coach, both in sports and in corporate settings. The icing on the cake in this book are the verses that bring those life lessons to … life!

Krishna Kumar has let the story do the work. A story that is sure to uplift you.

ND Badrinath, Media & Market Research Guru, Published Author, Mumbai (India)

A book that has enduring significance and contains authentic wisdom and teaching, rather than being a temporary 'fad', is a rare discovery and gift. Krishna Kumar's **Crossing the Rubicon** – *Wisdom Trails with the Old Monk*, is such a book. The reader is taken on a wonderful, enlightening journey of self-discovery. The 'path' travelled may not be far, but very much within ourselves, where the answers may always have rested. The Old Monk has always been with us, and his lessons have been 'taught' many times over the millennia; but his wisdom is too often forgotten and 'lost' over time, awaiting re-discovery. Our own age is one that has great need of the Old Monk's wisdom and guidance, so we may find better paths to travel that get us back on more fruitful tracks. This is a book you can carry with you always; a treasured text whose quiet wisdom will never fail to inspire and guide the reader.

Philip Beddows, International Coach & Mentor, Founder, The Silk Road Partnership

For
my parents
Mani & Vasudevan
my first
Old Monks

Contents

Prologue *11*

Chapter 01   Meeting Old Monk 13
Chapter 02   The Hare's Tale 19
Chapter 03   The Bent Tree 21
Chapter 04   The Resilient Rose 30
Chapter 05   The Honest Hypocrite 31
Chapter 06   The Mask 40
Chapter 07   The Quixotic Dreamer 42
Chapter 08   Alter Ego 50
Chapter 09   Conversations Aren't Happenstance 52
Chapter 10   Silence Speaks 62
Chapter 11   Crossing the Rubicon 64
Chapter 12   The Inner Devil 73
Chapter 13   The Seeker 76
Chapter 14   Who is the Old Monk 85
Chapter 15   The Virtuous Life 86
Chapter 16   The Eagle in My Soul 94

Epilogue *95*
Acknowledgements *97*
About the Author *98*

Prologue

Dear Reader,
At the very outset, you will meet someone special.

One who is seemingly enigmatic but all too real, one who will fascinate you while engaging you in conversation, leaving you lost in self-reflection.

That's the Old Monk.

> In the mountains lies a special brewery,
> A destination for the cognoscenti.
> Where you'll meet man's truest friend,
> An Old Monk, a druid, the stuff of legend.
> He brews an elixir to quench the driest thirst,
> Has a recipe that overcomes life at its worst.
> A mix of cinnamon and vanilla, a dash of lime.
> All garnished with a hint of mint or thyme.
> One that will send warmth up any spine,
> Beat the best of any ambrosia or wine.
> A sip and you scream, "a man's come of age,"
> Ready for battle on the big stage.
> But for distilling that euphoric blend,
> Old Monk uses a special ingredient,
> One that's tough to comprehend,
> Hidden as your soul's deepest intent.

As you journey through these pages, dear Reader, you are encouraged to step back, pause a few moments, and reflect on your own journey through life.

Ask yourself if the Old Monk's wisdom leaves you with subliminal messages that point you in the direction of newer and better paths as you travel through life.

Chapter 01

Meeting Old Monk

"**Y**ou seem to be in a hurry, my young friend," said the Old Monk. "Are you not aware that this path leads back to where you started out?"

And that's how the Chief first met the Old Monk, beginning a conversation between two strangers that would lead to transforming one of them forever.

What brought about this first meeting? Their story began many seasons ago. Call it serendipity.

Circling far above the clouds, the eagle sensed the onset of an impending monsoon shower. Her telescopic vision continually scanned the ground below. Briefly alighting atop a sky-high pine tree, she started a swift glide to the ground. Doubtless, her laser-sharp eyes had targeted a tasty prey to feed her offspring.

Unknown to the eagle, a Himalayan wolf crouched in readiness to attack. The wolf had not fed for three long days and had its sights set on the same prey, a hare nibbling away alongside a small mountain trail. Neither the restless eagle nor the impatient wolf was aware that their next actions would be instrumental in shaping the lives and fortunes of countless individuals.

It may have been a shadow cast by the eagle in flight or a breeze that blew downwind from the wolf, but the hare, alarmed, swiftly bounded away from the attacking wolf. The eagle, distracted by the wolf running across her path, found herself unable to slow down her flight. Her razor-sharp talons, stretched in readiness to grab the hare, scraped the surface of the track, dislodging a few small rocks before she flew away.

Mountain trails are usually paths hewn and strengthened by loose stones and pebbles, cemented with wet mud. Strengthened by the many monsoon showers that followed, the spot where the small rocks had been dislodged by the eagle gradually formed a deceptively small but treacherous pothole.

It was the very spot where the Chief, speeding on his motorbike, lost control and swiped a gentle Old Monk on his morning walk off the path.

Most of us have met people like the Chief. They act as the barometer of success that every youngster wants to emulate. Oozing confidence, they wield influence in every corridor of power. They are the captains of industry, the actors who are superstars, the champion sportsperson, or even a combination of any of these and more.

Clearly, while every one of them doesn't always become a superstar or a champion, we would have met them in the course of our daily lives for the making of the Chief starts at a young age. Whether in school or university, in the workplace or our social circles, while many of their contemporaries are content to progress on a set path, they are the restless achievers pushing themselves continuously, holding onto the perception that 'there is so much to be done and so little time.'

If the eagle was urged by worry and restlessness, the wolf driven by hunger and impatience, it was the urgency of ambition that powers a Chief. An ambition that encourages speedy work, the need to be known as an achiever—while often leading to great success—can easily cast the shadow of hubris. Where winning in the workplace comes often at the cost of unhappiness in life--an epiphany that is often realised in the twilight of their lives.

Our Chief, like most of his ilk, would take an annual vacation with his family. The family would spend time relaxing in resorts located on beach fronts, go on a wildlife safari, or do tourism trips in historical cities. On this occasion, they were staying in a mountain resort. While the rest of his family were comfortably ensconced at the resort, 'relaxing' in the Chief's lexicon was best done with long drives at high speeds on mountain paths on his motorbike.

Though he considered these vacations as ways to recharge and renew himself, there were times when he wondered if that truly was the reason to step away from the hustle of daily living. Often, a niggling but persistent thought would pop up. Was there something missing in his approach to work and to life? Could there be more to his life than all that he was doing? When the answer proved elusive, he would brush aside these bothersome questions and get immersed in his work.

Watching the Old Monk pick himself up from the path where he had fallen, a contrite Chief stopped and rushed to help him. It was when he said, "Are you hurt? I am terribly sorry," that the Old Monk in a clear voice that was to resonate—then and forever—spoke the words that we read at the start of the story.

There was no hint of grumbling or admonishment in his voice. Only a gentle concern and—possibly—what the Chief believed was genuine curiosity.

Faced with the Old Monk's strange query after he had recovered from the fall, the Chief, rarely at a loss for words, found himself scrambling for a suitable reply.

"Yes, of course, I know where the road leads," he said. "Though, for me, the path is less important than the thrill of driving. I enjoy the feel of the wind on my face, the pulsating sound of my motorbike, and watching the forest flying past on both sides. It's a great experience, one that makes me come alive and feel refreshed."

"Why don't you join me on the rest of my walk," offered the Old Monk. "Perhaps you will discover another kind of experience, not dissimilar, though with an interesting difference."

On the verge of politely refusing the offer, for it wasn't in the Chief's character to break from his planned agenda, a residual feeling of guilt held him back from doing so. After all, he did owe the Old Monk for his graciousness. So, somewhat to his surprise, he heard himself accepting the offer.

Without another word, the Old Monk moved forward briskly, the Chief walking a few steps behind him. In a few minutes, they turned off the path onto a small trail that led deeper into the forest. They moved at a steady pace, but gradually the Chief found that he had to strain to keep up with the older man. He prided himself on being fit. After all, with three days a week of competitive tennis and another three days of rigorous workouts at his fitness club, he knew that he was in top shape. Why, then, was he tiring while the elderly sage seemed to move ahead so comfortably?

He noticed that the dense forest had thinned and the barely felt breeze shifted to a much stronger wind. The Chief's legs were hurting. As they had now arrived at a clearing, he was on the verge of asking for a break when the Old Monk abruptly stopped and motioned to the Chief to stand alongside him.

Though it was a mere three steps that took him next to the Old Monk, the entire atmosphere had changed. The wind was now blowing fiercely with a deafening sound. It took all his effort to maintain his balance and amidst it all, he heard the Old Monk's clear voice, "Don't look down, it is a sheer drop. Rather, look straight ahead."

The view ahead was stunning. Stretching for miles, the scene was majestic—grand and a visual delight. There was no movement except for a lone eagle that was circling. Caught up in the immensity of the panorama, the Chief momentarily forgot even his own existence. His worries, dreams, and emotions came to a standstill. Though he was standing on a cliff and a misstep would likely take him over the cliff's edge, he felt no fear.

The Old Monk spoke again, "Watch, even the mighty eagle in flight, records no trail that we sight. Often, the faster we go, the more we stand still."

"There is an interesting illustration to this wisdom," he continued, "you would have heard the oft-told fable of the Hare and the Tortoise. In the conventional tale, the swifter, though lazy, hare loses the race to the slow and steady tortoise. That isn't quite how the story ended. Someday, allow me to tell you what really happened."

These enigmatic words from the gentle sage captivated him. They captured his attention and left him wondering if there was a different path that he could pursue, another way of thinking. However, there was a part within the Chief that continued to remain sceptical, for it is very hard to discard a conditioned way of thinking. His curiosity was piqued, and he resolved to get the sage to share the Hare's Tale.

"That sounds fascinating. I would be delighted," said the Chief, "if you could tell me the Hare's Tale."

And so the Old Monk spoke of the truth behind the race run between the Tortoise and the Hare.

We are now left wondering if it was the actions of an eagle and a wolf, a quirk of fate, good karma, or pure coincidence that it was in the Chief's destiny to meet the Old Monk.

The Hare's Tale

Haven't you heard the tale of the merry hare?
Bounding around the forest with scarcely a care,
Proud of his fame as the fastest in a race,
Till challenged to beat the tortoise in a race.

The confident hare, the story goes, took a nap,
Woke when his plodding foe was on the final lap,
That set the stage for the fable to have a moral,
Slow and steady is the way to win the laurel.

Don't stop at history that's inscribed by the victor,
Their tactics aren't always a success predictor,
It would be good to know what the hare went through,
Mightn't the loser have learned a lesson or two?

When I met this famous hare one sunny day,
Curiously, he seemed to show little dismay.
"Yes," said he, "one might say that's a race I lost,
In truth, it was all about my opportunity cost.

That day, as I awoke from beneath the oak,
Knew my few leaps would pass the slowpoke,
What froze my feet then was the thought,
Would the prize of winning end as nought?

The burden of expectation is heavy to bear,
A champ must always be ready for many a dare,
A challenge by a cheetah or gazelle may be won,
But there'll be a day when I am fully outdone.

So, friend, the epiphany that shook me awake,
Was that some races are best to forsake,
Life isn't lived through a continuous chase,
Success comes by setting one's own pace."

Chapter 03

The Bent Tree

The Old Monk abruptly stopped walking when he reached a strangely shaped tree.

Though the tree stood alone in the clearing, it was clear from the scattered tree trunks around that there had been many others growing in the same spot at some time. While in a forest that abounds with trees of all types and sizes, a lone tree is bound to stand out, this one seemed to have a peculiar shape that was bound to catch the eye.

Before we proceed, let's take a moment to understand how the Old Monk and the Chief found themselves at the tree.

After his brief encounter with the elderly sage, the Chief found himself often revisiting and ruminating over their conversation. All day, he found himself in a disturbed state of mind, and sleep eluded him through much of the night. Thus, it was hardly surprising that the following morning, he drove on his motorbike through the same path, though at a far slower pace, hoping to meet the Old Monk again. He hoped that the Monk, like himself, would be a creature of habit and follow the same route on his daily walk.

He was to be disappointed, for he couldn't see the sage anywhere along the path despite driving on the same route more than once. After a while, feeling a little disgruntled, he decided to turn back. Maybe he would have to postpone meeting the Old Monk to another day.

That thought did little to lessen his irritation. His ruminations, sadly, seemed to have become worse, and the rest of the morning found him wandering about in a sullen mood. In the afternoon, increasingly restless, he decided to take a short walk to clear his head.

Barely had he turned the corner, when he saw the Old Monk serenely perched on a boulder alongside the road as though he had been waiting for him all the time.

"You seem disturbed today, my young friend," was how the Old Monk started the conversation.

"Old Monk—if you will allow me to call you by that name—that is indeed true. When you walked me to the edge of the cliff yesterday, I was so absorbed in the beauty and majesty of the mountains looming ahead that I was momentarily freed from all my worries. That was a wonderful feeling. Then, in a short while, all my problems came flooding right back, messing with my head. It is in moments like these that I begin to wonder if I am on the right track, following the right path," confessed the Chief.

He looked confused, even as he was posing his query to the Old Monk. Though he desperately wanted the answer to a question that had been eluding him for a long time, he held the secret hope that the old sage would justify his scepticism by failing to do so.

"In all honesty, I thought I had it all figured out, Old Monk. For the longest time, there was never the slightest doubt in my mind about the direction I was taking," the Chief sighed, rubbing his temple. "But there are times nowadays when I feel like I'm stumbling in the wrong direction. That I am gradually losing my way, and something is missing in my plan. How do I again start believing that I am on the right way?"

The Old Monk gazed at him thoughtfully; his eyes twinkling with quiet curiosity. He replied, "Despite all our planning, is the journey of life ever a straight one? Aren't the twists and turns, though some may be daunting, what makes our path and defines our path? So, can being lost really be such a bad thing, when most of us never truly know where we're headed from the start?"

The Chief wasn't convinced. "And what if these unexpected turns make things worse? They force my hand and make me take the wrong decision. If I fail, that will mean I made the wrong choice, wouldn't it?"

"Yet.. is there really such a thing as a 'wrong' choice?" the Old Monk smiled, his head tilted to one side, giving him a mischievous look. The Chief would soon come to know that these were the tricky moments when the sage would put forward a seemingly innocent question but one that demanded deep introspection.

"Do join me on my walk. I would like to take you somewhere that might help you work out your path when there is neither a right nor a wrong one," continued the Old Monk.

They walked slowly together.

The Chief realised that he was gradually falling into the same pattern of walking set by the Old Monk. The pace was a measured one, very different from his usual style, nevertheless it felt comfortable. He also found that his restlessness was easing. He was now able to think in a far more detached way.

The late afternoon shadows merged, bringing the forest back to life. The route took them past densely wooded areas, and the Chief sensed that it wasn't a path that was used regularly. The Old Monk was silent, allowing the Chief to continue with his reflections and enjoy the scenic beauty around them.

The Old Monk finally spoke after pausing at the bent tree. "As this is a path that I frequently walk on, I can bear witness to the history of the tree that you see before us. In its early days, this tree, like many of its brethren, was young and fragile. When the first storm hit, the tree bent under the pressure of fierce winds, its branches swaying and its trunk leaning to withstand the force. Yet, unlike many of the others that struggled to stay upright, it endured the harsh conditions, absorbing the rain and permitting itself to bend till the storm eventually blew itself out. Where the other trees who fought to stay upright now remain only as bare trunks, our tree though bent survived, its roots digging deeper into the soil, securing its foundation.

As the years went by, I watched the bent tree gradually grow taller and stronger. Despite now standing alone in a wide clearing, exposed to the elements, it had built an inner resilience, toughened by every experience. Each storm has added to its strength, each gust of wind moulded its branches, giving them character. Where its bark was once smooth, it is now rugged and weathered, a testament to the challenges faced and overcome.

Today, I treat this tree as a symbol of endurance. Its sturdy trunk is a monument to its perseverance, and its tall, far-reaching branches signify growth beyond adversity. The tree, though bent, still sways gracefully in the wind, unafraid of the storms to come, for it has proven its ability to survive, thrive, and stand firm despite the challenges it has faced."

It was a simple anecdote, though deep in meaning. While no doubt, other trees in the forest would also have weathered the storms, the Chief felt drawn towards the magnificent symbol of resilience in front of him. Silent, lost in contemplation, his brow furrowing in thought, he pondered the reason for the Old Monk bringing him to the tree. It took him a while to respond.

"Maybe," he said after a while, "the lesson that the bent tree teaches us is that wanting to stay in control is not the answer to avoiding failure. I am convinced that it was my fear of failing that made me want to stay in control." He seemed almost vulnerable, caught between the pressures of responsibility and the nagging fear of failure. It wasn't just the weight of the decisions he had made, but the ones he hadn't—the unknown paths, the opportunities missed, the mistakes that still lingered in the back of his mind.

The Old Monk raised an eyebrow as if pondering the Chief's words.

"Control," he murmured. "Can we ever truly have it? Often, the desire to stay in control is our defence against feelings of self-doubt that keep cropping up. I am sure that on many occasions when we were able to successfully navigate through uncertainty, it was because, like the bent tree, we were comfortable to relinquish control and rather trusted in ourselves."

"Trusting myself, that's easier said than done," retorted the Chief, a hint of frustration creeping into his voice. His eyes darted upwards for a moment as if seeking solace from the bent tree.

"Moreover, when I find myself moving on the wrong path…" his words trailed off, betraying the unease he tried so hard to mask. A heavy sigh followed, the weight of doubt hanging in the air. He clasped his hands tightly so as not to betray a deeper sense of uncertainty that was creeping in. Despite his many years of leadership and the countless decisions that had brought him to this moment, these were the moments of self-doubt that preyed on him like an itch that needed to be continually soothed.

The Old Monk's eyes permitted himself another smile. Patiently he added, "And what if you've never left the right path, but just didn't know it? Suppose we convert every element of uncertainty in our journey to an exciting adventure, then rather than being perturbed, we would happily allow them to unfold as we moved ahead?"

The Chief wasn't convinced. All his life, he had been conditioned to plan for contingencies and be prepared to overcome them as and when they occurred. "Still it's unsettling," he mumbled, frustration creeping into his voice. "If I start with a clear plan, and then it feels like I'm fumbling in the dark, it will be hard to let go of my need to know what's ahead of me."

The Old Monk nodded slowly. "Hmm… darkness doesn't always mean that you are off course. It might simply mean that the path has shifted. When a flowing river encounters a boulder, instead of stopping to flow or forcing it off the path, it finds a way to flow around it. Rather than clinging to following a map, what if we learned to flow like the river, even when the waters are cloudy?"

It was the Chief's turn to permit himself a smile. "So, I just keep moving forward, ignoring the possibility of making the wrong decision, even if I'm not sure where I'm going."

The Old Monk met the Chief's smile with one of his own. He sensed that their conversation had moved in the direction of relaxed dialogue, a shift from being interrogative to inquisitive.

"What if that's enough for now?" he countered in a softer tone. "What if the path reveals itself only as we walk it? Each step, uncertain as it may be, could have its own purpose. Is there any decision that can't teach us something? Every road that we take brings with it its own lessons, and whenever we stray, there is safety in knowing that the way back is always there. Perhaps the paths we take through life are more forgiving than we think."

"What if the plan was never meant to stay fixed?" he continued. "Must we see the whole road to keep moving forward? It is much easier when we accept that life never really hands us all the answers from the start."

Lost in thought, the Chief finally said, "I hadn't thought of it quite that way. I guess I'm always trying to plan too far ahead and getting perturbed by problems whenever they arise."

The Old Monk gazed out towards the horizon, drawing the Chief's gaze once more to the majesty of the mountains. The silence enfolded them.

Slowly, the Old Monk turned back to the Chief with a knowing look. "When we try to imagine, to live in a future that is yet to arrive, isn't that where much of our worry begins? Wouldn't it be better to believe that the path we are traversing is the right one? That it is in front of us, waiting to be fully experienced. Once we accept it, only then can we find the beauty in every movement we make, that we start feeling alive at the moment, rather than waiting for a feeling of accomplishment at our journey's end."

The Chief had always believed himself to be a man of action. His approach to dealing with problems and challenging situations was to meet them head-on. It was an approach that had, so far, always succeeded, but now, the Old Monk had drawn him into a more philosophical, questioning frame of thought. He sensed that there was a gradual shift in his thinking, though he wasn't quite certain whether it was one that would help him.

"I understand, Old Monk, why you brought me to this spot. I too have weathered many a storm by attempting to have the elements work for me," the Chief's voice was quieter now, as though speaking more to himself than to anyone else. "Yet now… this is different. It is as though there is a different kind of storm brewing within me and like the roots of the bent tree, the resolve and strength to overcome also lies deep inside myself. In fact, I am reminded of a poem that I studied as a child about a rose bush, which has a lot in common with the bent tree."

Once he had recited the poem from memory to the Old Monk, he knew that this was their first dialogue, and it wasn't going to be their last. It had been an engrossing time and had firmed his resolve to continue meeting with the Old Monk, without leaving their get-togethers to chance.

Thus, when they parted, they planned to meet again the next day at the very same spot.

"Wanderer, your footsteps are the road, and nothing more;
wanderer, there is no road, the road is made by walking. By walking
one makes the road, and upon glancing behind one sees the path
that never will be trod again. Wanderer, there is no road—Only
wakes upon the sea."
– Antonio Machado

Chapter 04

The Resilient Rose

Here and there, rose bushes everywhere.
Shining softly in the midsummer glare.
Hidden in their midst, though, is a single bush,
That seems in need of a powerful push.

On her feeble branches, no roses bloom,
Not in her fate to release a soft perfume.
Will she be destined to live in gloom?
Unseen, unheralded from womb to tomb?

Two score and ten days have passed,
The roses are plucked, the bushes look dead,
But wait, our single bush now stands strong.
It bloomed late and will blossom year-round.

Is that not a feature we often find?
Where some win and others are forgotten.
Fortune, though, smiles on a rare few,
Who battle the odds and break through.

Chapter 05

The Honest Hypocrite

"I wonder," the Old Monk enquired quizzically of the Chief, "if you have heard about a literary personality called Polonius. He plays a prominent role in the famous Shakespearean play, Hamlet."

When recalling Polonius, the Old Monk was responding to a question that the Chief had posed to him almost immediately when they met the next day under the welcoming shade of the bent tree.

"I've noticed," grumbled the Chief, "that we often get so caught up in trying to please others and conform to the roles society expects us to play that we soon adopt a series of fake personas. In time, we are unable to discern between our 'pretend' self from our true self. Won't that lead to us living an inauthentic and ultimately unhappy life?"

Clearly, it was a question that had been bothering the Chief for a long time. While waiting for the Old Monk to reply, his mind wandered to when he had first been struck by this thought.

The atmosphere prevalent in the meeting room was gloomy, much like the day was cloudy outside. Desperately trying to close a critical business deal, the Chief had reached his wits' end for the negotiations that had dragged on for months and showed no signs of a conclusion.

On the contrary, it seemed that the tension in the room was at a peak with the other side not budging from their position. The Chief sat waiting for something—anything—that could help break the stalemate. He had hoped that it would be the final meeting, the moment where everything came together but the communication continued to be peppered with vague replies, routinely deferring decisions that could bring the deal to a close. Where he had hoped that the result of the meeting would begin a new era of growth and leapfrog his business, instead, he had left the room with a sense of unhappiness that went far beyond mere frustration.

Though sitting comfortably at home later that evening, bathed in the soft glow of dusk, the Chief remained in an unsettled state. He knew that something about the meeting earlier that day was bothering him, beyond the superficial conversation that had taken place. Yes, he reflected, all through the meeting, the conversation had seesawed from mundane business topics to thornier, more controversial matters. There were times when both sides had been aggressive, followed by moments of conciliation. On an occasion, a surprising display of empathy had emerged, but it was fleeting. What gnawed at the Chief, though, was the realisation that he had been so focused on closing the deal that he had, on more than one occasion, altered his approach to fit what he thought the client wanted to see. The more he pondered, the more uneasy he became. Somewhere along the way, his instinct told him that he had stopped being himself, all in the name of attempting to force a favourable outcome.

It was a troubling realisation that throughout the negotiation he had been slipping in and out of different roles, as if trying on, wearing and discarding a set of masks to shield his true feelings.

Why had he been wearing and hiding behind these masks, he asked himself? Was it because he craved the other's approval or to cover up a deeper sense of inadequacy? Did he need another person's validation to feel successful? What if someone saw through the masks he kept switching and wearing, wouldn't he be considered fake or worse, a fraud? Why the pretence, he wondered?

So, carrying the weight of doubt, with a niggling feeling of inadequacy, the Chief had asked the question to the Old Monk. Though he would later confess that the old sage's reply had caught him unawares. Over time, he observed that it was a pattern adopted by the Old Monk to deal with an immediate problem by approaching it through a different path.

"I am intrigued by your reference to the famous play, Hamlet," he responded. "Indeed, it was a classic tome that I had studied while at school, though it is tough to recall all the characters in detail at this time."

"While penning Hamlet, in sketching out the roles portrayed by the various actors in the play, one can see the genius of William Shakespeare," continued the Old Monk, "There is no doubt that Shakespeare had a deep understanding of human behaviour that he applied while creating his characters. Take our interest in Polonius, who is the adviser to the key villain Claudius. He features as a multifaceted character donning several contrasting, some despised, roles including those of a wise old man, a devious politician, and a manipulator of his children. In the end, he was shown as a scapegoat, a self-absorbed fool. The intriguing question to ponder is that while fleshing out the character of Polonius was Shakespeare drawing to our attention that, like Polonius, we also play multiple roles as we move through life?"

"Polonius does sound like a fascinating character, Old Monk," said the Chief. "Even so shouldn't we be fair to him, make allowances that he was probably forced to get into these personas to deal with the situations that were thrown at him."

He continued, "In Polonius, I can see a distinct resemblance with many individuals with whom I have interacted. They, either driven by their own expectations or a desire to conform to those set by the wider society, end up creating for themselves a distinct personality. For example, those leaders who want to be viewed as ambitious, result-oriented, and tough negotiators will strive to portray that impression, often burying their natural impulse to respond differently. When someone behaves in a manner that is inconsistent with who they really are, then even when they achieve the desired outcomes, they run the risk of wondering if their success was a stroke of luck rather than a measure of their own ability. It is a pattern of behaviour that is now labelled as the 'Impostor Syndrome.'

Hence, I return to my original question. If the hallmark of one's true self is authenticity, that of being true to oneself, then shouldn't they stop wearing masks?"

"Isn't that the question you should be asking yourself?" the Old Monk replied, his voice gentle but probing. "Do you feel like the masks you wear are distancing you from who you really are, what you want to achieve? And if they are, can you still be true to yourself without discarding them?"

The Chief sat quietly. The two of them had moved and were now seated facing each other. They sat on adjacent tree trunks, two among the many that were scattered around the bent tree. There was something, he thought, in the Old Monk's words that resonated deeply within him. He realised that during the negotiations, in his keenness to succeed by closing the deal, he had been trying to accommodate the others, he had moulded himself into someone he wasn't and, in the process, felt that he was gradually losing his sense of self-worth.

When he shared this insight, the Old Monk's face broke into a broad smile. Soon, the Chief would begin to enjoy this gesture as it carried with it a sense of encouragement. "To be able to detach from one's created persona, the removal of masks must begin with an awareness that one is not being truly authentic in interactions with others. It is possibly the hardest step, for there will be a reluctance to step outside the comfort of one's artificially created 'safe' identity. However, only by first recognising this negative aspect of our behaviour can we move forward to overcome it. I am delighted that you applied mindfulness to move your thoughts, shifting them from an external affirmation of your self-worth to an internal acceptance."

"Thanks. That is very encouraging to hear, but I must confess that in this instance my insight or level of awareness might be a fluke. Are there any critical signs that I can watch out for, observe, indicating that a mask was being slipped on?" inquired the Chief.

"Yes, that's true, most times people do struggle to recognise their created persona." The Old Monk had switched to a rare prescriptive approach. "May I suggest some typical signs or signals that help to identify the masks that we wear? Consider the situation that you had spoken about when you described your difficult negotiation situation that needed a successful outcome. At any point, did you stop, pause, and reflect on whether the deal that you were working hard to close wasn't only about growing your business but more about seeking external recognition, that you wanted your success to gain you accolades from the peer network?"

The Chief was taken aback. The Old Monk's query was hard-hitting. Though, he reflected wryly that he brought it upon himself and so, laughing, he responded, "If you had asked me that question a few days ago, I would have been indignant. Now, I can sense that you are holding up a mirror to look within myself. Thank you!"

"What's more," the Chief continued, "I am encouraged to delve deeper and identify another situation where my fake persona might have been at play. For instance, a week ago, I relaxed some of our business regulations ostensibly to improve morale. It is possible, though, that my hidden purpose was to improve my popularity within the team."

"Once again, I admire your ability to introspect and identify another situation that challenged you to stay true to your character while being subtly influenced to don a different role," the Old Monk continued to smile.

"Well, it's fascinating how the persona we show isn't really who we are at the core." The Chief's thoughts were now in full flow. "It's more of a social façade, shaped partly by what society demands from us—like the roles we play at work, with family, or in social situations. However, it's also influenced by what we personally aspire to be. We shape our persona to meet both social expectations and our own ambitions. So, we are caught in a bind of constantly balancing the pressure to fit in with what society wants and what we want to project about ourselves."

"Exactly," concurred the Old Monk. "Nevertheless here's where it gets even more complicated. According to the famous psychologist, Carl Jung, there's another part of us, deep down, that is hungry for and craves individuality and autonomy. That's our internal drive to be unique, to express who we really are. As a result, while one part of us is working to belong, there's another part that is pushing back, seeking an outlet for personal freedom and self-expression.

"Isn't that conflicting, paradoxical?" the Chief sounded confused. "There's a part of us that's trying to fit in, and another part that is pushing to stand out and be noticed."

"Yes, that is a paradox, especially for people who are in the spotlight, like actors, champions in sports, and business leaders," commented the Old Monk. "They're constantly balancing their need to assert individuality alongside the pressure to conform to social and organisational expectations. That's why they sometimes actively seek recognition or fame—they're trying to be unique but equally desire acceptance from their peer network and society. It's a constant push and pull that's tough to navigate."

"It is falling into place, making sense. Well, it's interesting how the persona we show isn't really who we are at the core. Hence, they have to juggle, to maintain the delicate balance by playing the roles society expects of them, while still wanting to assert individuality," summarised the Chief.

"You have captured the essence of the paradox very neatly," applauded the Old Monk. However, he quickly moved ahead by adding another dimension. "There is another important issue that arises from donning masks. The inherent danger while wearing masks is that, over time, they become increasingly tough to peel away. By continually adopting a 'fake' persona, by acting hypocritically, we dilute our authenticity. In time, we adopt the false persona and are gradually separated from our True Self. In the spirit of the paradox, I have labelled this character as the 'Honest Hypocrite', you may be amused to know."

It was a curious turn of phrase that made them both pause and smile.

"How, then, can we not drape a fake persona," asked the Chief, "and remain our authentic selves?"

"Perhaps, the answer again is found in reading Hamlet," pronounced the Old Monk. "Shakespeare gave Polonius a myriad of roles, but he also had him realise the dangers in being the 'honest hypocrite'. It is as early as Scene 3 in the First Act of Hamlet that Polonius advises his son, Laertes, "To thine own self be true, and it must follow, as the night the day, thou canst not then be false to any man."

The Old Monk must have sensed that the Chief had found an answer to his dilemma, for there was no further discussion. The Chief was flattered when the wise sage invited him to drop in at his house the following day.

A few weeks later, during the next round of negotiations with the same persons, the Chief realised something was different. He understood that his talk with the Old Monk had made him acutely aware of his reactions. He started to detect a definite change in his approach, not allowing himself to be provoked or trying to be too accommodating. He caught himself before slipping into another mask, grounding his responses in what truly mattered: the goal of the deal, not the need for approval. He stayed focused, allowing the conversation to flow naturally. There was no pretence, no shifting of roles, just clarity. Not being drawn to pulling on a mask helped him maintain his composure and a feeling of freedom. Interestingly, he realised that there was a shift in the momentum in his direction as though freeing his potential had energised the atmosphere. It wasn't long before the dialogue was harmonious and ended in a successful closure of the deal.

As he left the room, the Chief whispered a silent thanks for the wisdom proffered by the Old Monk.

"The greatest battle we face as human beings is the battle to protect our true selves from the self the world wants us to become."
– E. E. Cummings

Chapter 06

The Mask

As time marches through a single day,
We don identities for the parts we play,
Personas that are but an effort to please,
In settings where we don't feel at ease.
A lurking impostor that peeps out in fear,
Playing out a masquerade to appear sincere,
That makes us spend many nights awake,
Worrying when we will be labelled as fake.

When our concerns cause concealing,
Masks adorn us in unappealing shapes.
Peeled, these masks leave no traces,
Are we, Old Monk, a result of myriad faces?

Wearing masks, Chief, keeps us safe,
Blocks our true self from freedom to grow,
Don't live watching how the wind blows,
It's tiring to switch from pose to pose.

Discarding masks can bring much relief,
Helps turn over a new leaf, strengthen belief,
Potential resides deep within the mind's shelf,
In the collective unconscious, our self.

Build your identity drawing on the psyche,
It balances our self, frees potential's key,
The fortunate few tap into its rich source,
Others, unknowingly, let it run its course.

"I only wanted to remain true to my own self. Why is it so difficult?"
– Hermann Hesse

Chapter 07

The Quixotic Dreamer

It was a nondescript book, lying open on the table, that first caught his eye.

The Chief was visiting the Old Monk's cottage for the first time. He was pleasantly surprised to find that, contrary to the sparse belongings usually found in monastic rooms, the Old Monk's home exuded all that was necessary to provide quality comfort and warmth. The furniture, clearly made of excellent quality, blended in well with the cottage-style surroundings.

Before the Chief's eyes could absorb the ambience and the various items in the room, he was arrested when he caught sight of the book. Bulky, bound in a vintage leather cover, it appeared to have been well-thumbed with markers holding many of the pages together. Intrigued, he wondered about the contents, but he was standing at too far a distance from the table to read either the title or decipher any of the words.

The Old Monk was perceptive.

"I guess you are curious to know about the book," said the Old Monk. "If that's true, you are in excellent company, for it is a book that has captivated readers for many hundreds of years. In fact, it is known to be the second most sold book in the world." Not to keep the Chief guessing, he continued, "What you are looking at is one of the earliest known editions of the classic 17th-century novel, Don Quixote, penned by Miguel de Cervantes. May I ask if you have read it?"

When the Chief admitted that he had only vaguely heard about the book, much less read it, the Old Monk continued, "The book is based on a fascinating theme that centres around the consequences of self-delusion. The novel has as its main protagonist a middle-aged nobleman named Alonso Quixano who has become obsessed with the ideals touted in the numerous books on chivalry that he has read. Renaming himself by the nobler name of Don Quixote de la Mancha, he sets out as a knight-errant on a quest to revive the lost virtue of chivalry. As the story progresses in the distorted reality of the illusionary world that Don Quixote now occupies, inns appear as castles, windmills become giants, and flocks of sheep look like armies that he must battle to restore his honour and serve the nation."

Captivated, the Chief urged the Old Monk to continue with his summary of the age-old tale. From their previous meetings, he had learned that the simplest chats with the Old Monk could take the inevitable route to deeper, powerful discussions.

"On his travels," continued the Old Monk, "Don Quixote is accompanied by his faithful squire, the peasant Sancho Panza, whose personality is cleverly created by Manuel Cervantes as a perfect foil to that of his master. Sancho Panza is not only physically the opposite of the tall, thin, sharp-featured Don Quixote, but his personality is based on common sense and reality. He often gently reminds his master about the real world using earthy proverbs that, unsurprisingly, infuriate the other man. Lest one wonders why Sancho Panza would choose to follow someone like

Don Quixote, the answer is that the latter has promised to better his humble lot with the temptation of being appointed as the Governor of a province."

"Indeed, a fascinating theme," admitted the Chief. "I am intrigued that, only yesterday, we were exploring the theme of wearing masks in our efforts to please others, attempting to map ourselves onto another person's reality. Today, the topic is moving in the diametrically opposite direction, that of distorting our own reality. Don Quixote, in this instance, creates an alter ego that feeds on his dreams, setting him on a path that would, I am guessing, end with him falling prey to self-delusion."

"Indeed, you have deduced the story's end quite accurately," concurred the Old Monk. "It does happen that we are often the victims of our own imagination, taking on far more than we can deal with. Before we continue, may I offer you some herbal tea? I must add that all the ingredients are homegrown. My visitors speak highly of its refreshing qualities."

In the cold mountain weather, a cup of tea was a welcome offering, and when the Chief gratefully accepted, the Old Monk busied himself preparing the brew.

In this brief hiatus, the Chief's mind wandered as he recalled chatting with a childhood buddy, a never-say-die sports champion. A few months ago, they were sitting in a café and Buddy, the eternal optimist from the time that Chief knew him, was the friend who was always on the move, ever challenging himself, hungry for winning and success. However, the Chief was concerned as he knew from their mutual friends that Buddy had been struggling for many months with results in his tournaments.

"Buddy, I know how passionate you are about your sport, but I had heard that you have run into a very bad patch, that things just aren't getting better. Have you thought about moving on, trying something different?"

"It is true that lately, I haven't had good results," Buddy reacted defensively. "Every player, even the greatest of champions, goes through downturns. I only need to weather this storm. I am confident that if I can win a couple more tournaments in the next few months, the turnaround will happen. After all, there are tons of success stories where things turned around, so I am confident mine will, too."

Listening to Buddy, the Chief realised that he was blinding himself to the harsh reality of his circumstances, clutching at straws and operating under the delusion that his struggles were temporary. By mentioning stories of other sports champions who had successfully overcome hardships, it was obvious that he was surviving on false hope and finding solace in selective optimism.

"Do you remember that's exactly what you said when we last met, almost six months ago?" The Chief had persisted. "Maybe it's time to step back and see if there's a deeper issue."

Buddy had remained obstinate. "No, all I need is one good run of victories. I can feel that it is right around the corner. Besides, I've invested too much already and sacrificed a lot—money, time, and energy. I can't walk away now and let it all go to waste."

Again, it was all too obvious that the thought of quitting felt unbearable. It would mean admitting that all his past efforts were in vain. The Chief took the gentler approach by stating, "I know it's hard to let go, but sometimes holding on too tightly to something that's not working can hurt you more in the long run.

It is necessary to be conscious of what's real while chasing your hopes, wouldn't you agree?"

The Chief's heart sank when Buddy retorted, "Don't worry. You'll see, it'll all pay off soon."

Today, in the light of the Old Monk's summary of the classic, reflecting on their chat, the Chief was able to find a parallel—Buddy was mirroring Don Quixote, while he had played the role of the pragmatic Sancho Panza—unsuccessfully attempting to shield his friend, who was trapped in a cycle of denial and unrealistic hope, from staying on the painful path to failure.

He shook his head, as if trying to let go of this unhappy memory, and reached his hand out to accept the tea that was being offered to him.

True to his word, the Old Monk's tea tasted delicious. As they sat, gently sipping on the hot brew, the Chief couldn't resist sharing his recent conversation with Buddy with the Old Monk.

"In your narrative, we can see Buddy exhibiting the typical 'dreamer's' personality," said the Old Monk. "I am not surprised that you saw the parallel with the behaviour of Miguel de Cervantes's protagonist, Don Quixote. Both are chasing dreams that seem out of reach or appear absurd to others. In their reality, though, they are the champions for the power of individuality, evangelising the chasing of one's dream, even in the face of societal ridicule.

We might go so far as to say that they have created an alter ego, one that makes them feel superhuman, to act like a superhero that takes on seemingly insurmountable challenges and saves the world."

"I am sure that such paths are rife with huge risks," interrupted the Chief. As one who was trained and conditioned to evaluate pitfalls, he wasn't comfortable with the turn that the conversation was taking.

"However, such persons do encounter several pitfalls that stem from their disconnection from reality," the Old Monk nodded. He went on, "If, like Buddy, their relentless pursuit of dreams blinds them to the practicalities of life, it can lead to a series of misguided and often rash actions. An inability to distinguish between passion and reality can also result in poor judgement, for they will misinterpret situations and take unnecessary risks, endangering themselves and others."

"I must mention, Old Monk," countered the Chief, "that presenting two sides of their personality only makes me more confused about the 'dreamers' mindset. Are you implying that a 'quixotic' personality isn't so bad after all?"

"If we go back to my earlier words, I mentioned that ignoring reality runs the risk of self-deception and failure," clarified the Old Monk. "Quixote's refusal to adapt isolated him, and similarly, dreamers too risk alienation if they don't balance their vision with practical realities. To balance dreams with realism is the key."

"I would add," he continued, "that the 'quixotic' personality that you referred to is not confined to sports but can extend to artists, musicians, business leaders and others in various professions who pursue their dreams in the face of adversity."

"The part that captivates me the most," confessed the Chief, "is when you refer to an alter ego. I am assuming that an alter ego is like a second identity or personality someone adopts. It lets them show a different side of themselves—like when superheroes have secret identities—or present a more ideal or exaggerated version of themselves. Is it somewhat like being two people?"

"In a way, yes," the Old Monk agreed. "It helps people express traits or behaviours they might not show in everyday life. Their alter ego then provides the freedom and the avenue to explore different parts of their personality, to help navigate difficult situations, or to showcase aspects of their personality that they may otherwise suppress."

They were silent again. It was this last comment by the Old Monk that made the Chief wonder if he might not have spoken differently to Buddy. Rather than suggest that it was time for Buddy to consider a different route, shouldn't he have encouraged his friend to delve into his alter ego, to discover the best version of himself, a version that would help his career recover and succeed?

The Chief found himself transported to the days of his youth, a time when he was captivated by television episodes of Star Trek, dreaming of possibilities to travel in space. He recalled conversations with many of his friends from those days when they would excitedly share dreams and plans for changing the world. At that time, creating alter egos inspired by fictional heroes was more than just a pastime; it was a powerful way to connect with their dreams of making a real-world impact. Inspired by heroes and fictional characters who stand up for justice, protect the environment, or fight for equality, he could relate to how some of his friends became entrepreneurs, actors, and sports champions. In fact, many of them would passionately speak about how their mission, like their superheroes, was to pursue paths that could solve the world's problems and fuel real-world dreams of building a better future.

Where, he wondered wistfully, had those dreams gone?

"Now, you catch me brooding," the Chief said with a grin, "where is my alter ego? I recall, it must have been a long time ago, from my days as a young lad, when such alter egos flooded my dreams. I am now inspired to call them back."

They were both smiling now, enjoying, savouring a moment of camaraderie.

The Old Monk knew well that it wasn't a question for which the Chief was seeking an answer. He guessed that he already had it.

Succinctly captured by Don Quixote when he proclaimed, "I know who I am and who I may be if I choose."

Chapter 08

Alter Ego

Who wouldn't like to own an Alter Ego?
With the beauty of Aphrodite and Apollo,
Athena's wisdom, the brilliance of Janus,
Glorified by the majesty of Zeus?

In these Grecian tales, dreams take shape.
As easy as pinning on a superhero cape.
Become a Crusader, Avenger, or Black Knight,
With mystical powers to set our world right.

Heroic tales in myths make us feel strong,
Tempt us to move from where we belong.
Old Monk, in giving flight to our dreams,
Aren't we parodying an unreal theme?
"A broken-winged bird that cannot fly,
Is that dream in sleep, friend, you let die?
Content to anchor you in a comfort zone,
Fearful of taking a flight to unknown places.

Hold fast to your dream, stick to the plot,
Avoid feeling caught in a Gordian knot.
There's no escape for those who but dream at night,
Dreaming, when awake, ignites the light.

Dispel your shadow, shed the status quo,
Spread those wings, become your Alter Ego.
The day you begin to live your life's theme,
The universe unites, propels your dream."

*When you want something, all the universe conspires
in helping you to achieve it.
– Paulo Coelho*

Chapter 09

Conversations Aren't Happenstance

"I was wondering if having a conversation is more than just a skill; isn't it a form of art?"

These were the first words that the Chief spoke to the Old Monk as they sipped on their respective beverages. While leaving the Old Monk's home, the Chief, keen to reciprocate the sage's hospitality, had invited him the next day to a well-known café in the town. As he walked down to the café in the town square, the Chief reminisced about his recent conversations with the Old Monk. He mused about the strange course they had always taken, with him starting out with scepticism, moving to curiosity, then to a deeper awareness, and a final acceptance. There was also the epiphany that, despite his mild demeanour, the elderly sage had used his conversational mastery to subtly influence his thinking in numerous ways. Were there some tips, he wondered, that he might get the Old Monk to pass on that could help him in his future conversations?

"It is curious that you brought up the topic of conversation," said the Old Monk. "Humans as a species, I am sure you would have found out by now, are always yearning to communicate with our fellow beings. And that our conversations are usually a mix of verbal and body language, though often what the other person recollects are the words in the conversation. A word, wrongly used, could cause lasting damage to the relationship."

"Still, isn't it terribly hard," queried the Chief, "to make sure that we always select the right word for the right occasion?"

"Yes. To be able to select the right word for the right occasion, we need to know more about the situation in which the conversation is taking place," the Old Monk expanded on the theme. "First, it is important to realise that conversations can take place at more than one level. At its most basic level, the intention of conversing may be to merely transfer information, to conduct a simple transaction, or to share an opinion. Is it not interesting that even at this most basic level, people are often misunderstood?"

The Chief could easily relate to the statement. All too often, while passing on what he believed to be simple instructions or advice, he had been forced to rephrase or clarify his messages.

The Old Monk continued, "When we intend to move the conversation a step higher, for instance when we attempt to influence the other person to accept our point of view, it gets harder. In such situations, if we take the wrong approach to the conversation, there is a chance that the other person will resist our point of view, or worse, we run the risk of potentially alienating the other person."

When the Old Monk paused, the Chief's mind wandered to a recent Saturday afternoon when he had found himself grappling with a similar dilemma.

The scene was a much-awaited family gathering that had taken place a fortnight ago. His teenage cousin, who had just graduated from high school, whispered to him that he wanted to share, in confidence, the plans that he was making for his future education. Knowing his cousin had looked up to him for years as a mentor, the Chief was flattered to be taken into the youngster's confidence.

To his chagrin, he soon found himself caught in a bind. His cousin, rather than asking his opinion, bluntly stated that he was planning to take a gap year to 'explore life' rather than head straight to college. Although Chief acknowledged that times had changed since his own days at college, the young man's desire to explore 'life' as he termed it seemed a risky path to follow. At that time, with much difficulty, he had kept a poker face while gathering his thoughts and trying to find the most suitable response.

He was anxious that his cousin should feel heard and understood while wanting to emphasise the potential challenges of taking time off at such a crucial juncture in one's life. Though he felt an obligation to share some hard truths drawing from his own experience that he had faced after his graduation and how it had impacted his plans, he realised the need to be cautious. He knew that showing resistance to the younger person's idea could well bring about a strong reaction.

Setting aside the thought, "What a tough ending to the week," he wondered how he could get his cousin to accept his point of view while avoiding the risk of coming across as unsupportive or discouraging. With these worrisome thoughts floating through his mind, he remained unsure whether to adopt a gentle, supportive tone that risked sounding as though he approved entirely or to be direct and risk coming off as overly critical.

Unable to find the right words at that time, the Chief had requested his cousin to allow him time to mull over the idea during his forthcoming vacation.

The Chief, therefore, thought it was an opportune moment to sound out the Old Monk on how he might conduct his next conversation with his cousin, hopefully finding a way to blend honesty with compassion. A difficult, almost contrarian, approach to communicate in a manner that's both palatable and minimising any damage felt by the receiver, while at the same time not diminishing in its importance. It seemed a challenge that would test even the Old Monk's wisdom to put into practice.

He, therefore, explained the situation to the Old Monk, closing with an idiom that his grandmother had often advised the family, "a bitter pill is better swallowed in a sugar coating." It was a phrase he thought of as the family's own version of the words, "an iron fist in a velvet glove," attributed to the French Emperor, Napoleon Bonaparte. The quote implied that a firm, even damaging message was better conveyed wrapped in gentleness.

The Old Monk's response was insightful. "Would you not say that your challenge, the toughest part of the conversation, is your desire to persuade your cousin not to proceed with his idea? When you attempt to influence another person to your line of thought, it is then that you are taking the conversation to the next level."

"I am reminded," said the Old Monk, "of a movie, 'Twelve Angry Men', that I had seen many years ago. The story dramatically portrays the power of influencing through conversation. I wonder if you have watched it."

When the Chief shook his head, he continued, "The story is set as a gripping courtroom drama where a twelve-man jury is tasked with deciding the fate of a young defendant accused of murder. Initially, the overwhelming verdict by 11 of the jurors is to vote 'guilty' with the sole opposition coming from one of the jurors who urges the group to discuss the evidence more thoroughly.

It leads the group to engage in heated, often angry, debates. In their confrontations with one another, they gradually come face-to-face with their own prejudices and are forced to question their assumptions about the reliability of witnesses and evidence produced in the courtroom.

At one stage, for instance, another juror observes that the elderly witness, with 'a torn jacket' and 'dragging one leg,' who claimed to have seen the defendant flee the scene of the crime, might not have done so but deluded himself that it took place. The juror argues, *"He probably wanted to be recognised—recognised for something, anything."* Another juror now supports this idea, noting the inconsistency in the testimony.

This insight now prompts a previously convinced juror to reconsider, who asks, *"You mean... you think he might have lied?"* When the earlier juror clarifies, *"Not deliberately... nobody wants to feel unimportant,"* he is convinced by this reasoning and changes his vote to 'Not Guilty.' Over the course of the movie, we find this pattern repeated often until all the jurors conclude that the prosecution's case is weak, leading to a unanimous 'Not Guilty' verdict.

I found that the movie brilliantly illustrates how arguments can be influenced through masterful conversation. Do watch it when you can."

The storyline sounded fascinating. The Chief made a mental note to watch the movie at the earliest opportunity. As usual, he noticed that the Old Monk hadn't given advice but pointed out a direction that he could take. However, on this occasion, feeling a sense of urgency, he decided to persist with his query.

"Suppose as we would have wanted to, we were unable to get across a thorny point, failing to get the other person to accept our opinion or point of view," he pressed on, "wouldn't it be helpful to learn why this happens, wouldn't it be wise to get to the crux of many a conversation not ending unhappily?"

"Even when we perceive not to have succeeded in influencing someone, that does not necessarily leave a sense of angst or create unpleasantness," continued the Old Monk. "We may find that our perception remains just that, as a perception. The reality could be different. What is it that makes us believe that we have failed?"

"That's easy to notice," the Chief said, smiling. "On quite a few occasions after I have spoken, there is a lengthy silence from the other person, which, no doubt, implies a disagreement with my viewpoint. To my mind, silence is a polite way to signal gentle disapproval. It disturbs me, and so, more often than not, I feel compelled to speak and 'break' the silence."

"As you have discovered, conversing in an atmosphere of silence is harder than we think," the Old Monk expounded on the theme. "Our modern-day living is set within a cacophony of noise, a continuing conversation. When we find ourselves in quiet situations, there is a tendency to feel a sense of loss, isolation, or rejection that, in turn, breeds insecurity. At that point, we begin to feel out of control and anxious. Did you know that this 'fear of silence' has existed since ancient times? The Greeks used the word, Sedatephobia, to describe it using a combination of *Sedate* (silent or sleeping or dead) with *Phobos* (aversion, fear, or morbid fear)."

"Though it's a relief to know that it is a common problem, I am anxious to find out how we overcome this fear." the Chief asked with some anxiety.

"Every problem, when approached correctly, can be turned to our advantage. Silence, too," said the Old Monk, "can be turned to our advantage. Was it not Lao Tzu, the Chinese philosopher, who said that *'Silence is a source of great strength?'* Learn to embrace the quiet rather than try to overcome it. Have you not observed that even when there may be no sounds discernible to an external ear, our inner voices continue to speak to us? And it is these inner voices that create an opportunity for us to pause and reflect on situations and issues. In the stillness, we are closer to our thoughts, we can question our comfort, or otherwise, and heighten our levels of self-awareness."

"The 'sounds within silence' seem to be very powerful," the Chief, secretly pleased that he had coined this catchy phrase, went on, "I realise that it is in 'the lap of silence' that I discover new ways and paths. You have also made me appreciate that when the other person falls silent, it might be their way to self-discovery through self-reflection. That when directed inwards, our inner energy takes us to deeper levels of self-awareness and helps find answers to problems."

The Old Monk offered one of his rare smiles. Somehow, it always made the Chief feel like a young kid who had been rewarded by his teacher.

"Though it may sound paradoxical," said the Old Monk, "a successful conversation happens in an atmosphere of silence. It is a good idea to work towards creating it and benefit from the moments as they happen. The skill is in stepping back when the person falls silent during the conversation. It is the weak who feel the discomfort of silence, who struggle with conversations, while the confident person is intuitively aware of the power of silence and is very comfortable when this happens during the conversation."

"Thanks for the insights, Old Monk," the Chief was understandably delighted. "Though I am still left with one last question. You had mentioned that there are many levels to a conversation. We have spoken about two of these levels. Is there another higher level?"

"Indeed, there is one higher level in communication. Probably the most difficult one to achieve," stated the Old Monk.

"Permit me to elaborate. You are very likely to encounter this challenge when you next speak with your cousin. While conversing with him and attempting to change his point of view, you must be prepared that he might perceive your reaction as a hidden threat to his present or planned state. Is it not natural when confronted with a perceived threat that he would respond in a way that you might find negative or irrational? If not dealt with properly, it is very easy for a feeling of comfort to move to one of distrust. A fluid conversation can only happen when there is an environment of trust. And trust builds when there is a keen appreciation of the consequences and impact that the communication might have on the other person."

The Old Monk had rarely spoken before at such length. In the lengthy pause that followed, the Chief found that he was embracing the state of silence that they had only just spoken about. Gathering his thoughts, he spoke in a measured tone, attempting to quietly summarise the Old Monk's words, "What you are saying is that I should not take trust for granted, even though it is my cousin who is confiding in me. That it is necessary to make sure that the trust he has in me continues throughout our conversation, however tough the topic might be. That it is necessary for me to reflect on the likely repercussions, the possible reactions before conveying potentially unhappy news."

Much later, after leaving the café and walking back to his vacation home, the Chief could feel a sense of lightness. He knew that it was from the realisation that the forthcoming conversation with his young cousin had been sitting heavily on his mind and that this burden had now been lifted from his shoulders.

The conversational cues that he had learned from the Old Monk, he believed, would help him communicate his thoughts and feelings in a balanced manner. He decided to keep control of his emotions whenever he felt a sense of disquiet, to intuitively wait without interruption, and to encourage the silences. He would communicate with empathy and clarity, aiming to offer insight without undermining his cousin's sense of agency and excitement.

They had spent the rest of their evening in casual conversation. Though, on reflection, the Chief knew that there was little that was casual in talks with his mentor, for that was how he had now come to view the venerable sage.

"In the attitude of silence, the soul finds the path in a clearer light, and what is elusive and deceptive resolves itself into crystal clearness."
– Mahatma Gandhi

Chapter 10

Silence Speaks

Conversing isn't as easy as one might think,
Thoughtless comments cause quite a stink.
Words if spoken as emotion-laden thought,
Often expose a window to one's blind spot.

The way back if one's speech is outspoken,
It becomes tough when the connection is broken.
Ill-formed messages, like birds in a cage,
When freed, it will fly far to disengage.

Then it's quiet, the dialogue's at a full stop,
Might it be that the conversation was a flop?
The speakers, though, often feel distraught,
Worry about the other, an unhappy thought.

Humankind craves more than just company,
A need to feel valued in the eyes of many.
When words cease, it's cause for concern,
All that's heard is the ears starting to burn.

Like a vacuum in space, it sucks in empty air,
The gap's plugged, words spoken in despair.

Why do we feel the urge to shout?
When there's really nothing to drown out?

Silence isn't the absence of sound,
You'll often find it's the other way around.
Seeking and searching, curious for more,
Our mind is the culprit that chatters galore.

When the urge to talk is escaping solitude,
The heart stays silent, our words intrude,
Sounds, unbroken by bouts of silence,
Split wide the mind, striving for balance.

In the quietening of our cluttered mind,
The stillness speaks of thoughts left behind.
Relishing the moment, of a mind subdued,
We find the timeless amidst solitude.

A fluid conversation isn't happenstance,
It takes the form of a flowing dance.
Only thoughts peppered with perception,
Entices the other to strive for connection.

If your mouth is fed with that silver spoon,
Speech is in sync with a hidden, rich tune.
An inner spirit now directs your voice,
The heart moves, the lips find sounds to rejoice.

Chapter 11

Crossing the Rubicon

Crossing the Rubicon

As never before, the Chief could feel the passage of time. With less than two days of his vacation left, a sense of urgency gnawed at him. He couldn't shake the anxiety—had he absorbed all he had hoped to from the Old Monk? The clock was unforgiving, and the time left felt far too short to grasp the depth of wisdom still waiting to be uncovered. How could he make the most of these fleeting hours? The thought consumed him, every moment ticking by like a reminder of what might soon slip through his fingers. A normally calm person, it seemed strange for the Chief to find himself in this emotional state.

Controlling himself with an effort, he resolved to make the most of his time with his mentor. In particular, he would spend his next, and final, meeting with the Old Monk conversing on a topic that was most important, one might say critical, to his immediate future.

It had happened on a Thursday, a few hours before he left for his vacation. The Chief received news that there was an opportunity for him to take over as the Regional Head of a global company. The new role was a challenging one. It would require him to turn around a floundering organisation but also demanded that he relocate, with his family, to another country. On the one hand, it appeared to be a golden chance for the Chief to fast-track his career. Though the business he was asked to run wasn't doing well, if he were to make it succeed, it would add a huge feather to his cap and be a stepping stone to larger possibilities all over the world.

On the other hand, the relocation meant that his family's comfortable lifestyle would be disturbed. Among the many challenges present, there was a need for them to learn a new language, understand and adapt to a different culture, and be sensitive to the fragile political situation prevalent in that part of the world. While his young family had always been very supportive, he wondered if it was fair to subject them to a fresh set of challenges to further his career, especially when he was doing very well in his present engagement and taking the plunge would likely close the door to the possibility of coming back if the situation didn't work out as planned.

If he decided to forego the opportunity—he was all too aware that roles, such as this one, came rarely—he shouldn't have to regret, in hindsight, whichever path he decided to take.

Though in these past days, his faith in the Old Monk's wisdom had grown, the Chief wondered if there was a door that the venerable sage might open to show him the best way.

At the Old Monk's request, they were meeting again at the bent tree.

With anxiety gnawing within him, it wasn't long before the Chief described the dilemma that he was grappling with, concluding by asking, "What is it, Old Monk, that holds back a person from pursuing their dreams? In the situation that I have shared with you, I am unable to figure out if there is some form of fear that is preventing me from grabbing this terrific opportunity, one that many others in my position wouldn't have any hesitation in accepting. Why do I hesitate?"

A cryptic smile showed on the Old Monk's face. "Your present dilemma is easily understood when you become aware that you are grappling with your Inner Devil," he said. "We all harbour, within us, a creature that I have mischievously named the Inner Devil. When he manifests, it is to play our inner critic, that of being self-critical. His is an aggressive voice that intrudes on our thoughts by putting forward self-defeating prophecies. In this instance, the main goal of the Inner Devil seems to be to persuade you to rest content in your present state rather than risk challenging the status quo."

"An Inner Devil messing with my mind!" exclaimed the Chief. "That's a fascinating thought. To imagine that there's a part of my mind that acts like a hidden enemy out to derail my plans and actions."

"That's true. Whenever we find a stimulating path that has the scope to free our potential, a path that we are passionate about, that's when our Inner Devil gets to work. His method is to draw on our memory so that we start recalling past failures and unpleasant incidents. In a short while, our mind is filling up with self-doubt. Our thoughts are rooted in worrying about the pitfalls, and the various internal or external obstacles that could delay or stop progress on our path. Soon, our levels of uncertainty and anxiety increase, energy levels fall, and there is a reluctance, a hesitation, to move ahead."

The Chief was silent for a long time. It was clear that he was reflecting on this insight offered by the sage. When he spoke, it was in a measured voice, as though he had intuitively arrived at a deep insight. "I have noticed, Old Monk, that many millions of people live out their lives completely out of touch and blissfully unaware of their capabilities and true worth. At the one extreme, when they are not dealing with the numerous anxieties and stresses of fulfilling their daily obligations, they move to the other extreme of being passive, a state of listlessness and boredom that they mistake for relaxation. The average person is, therefore, spending his days either daydreaming of taking up projects (his passion) but letting them fly past or is stuck in the tedium of staying busy by frantically catching up on a set of endless tasks (his purpose)."

"That is indeed an astute observation," the Old Monk's words flowed. "The ancient Roman philosopher Seneca the Younger eloquently described this activity when he said, *'Their roaming is idle and pointless like ants crawling over bushes, which purposelessly make their way to the topmost branch and then all the way down again.'* Many people live a life like these creatures, and you could not unjustly call it busy idleness."

"Allow me to rephrase Seneca the Younger's words," the Chief appeared to have comfortably slipped into the role of the Old Monk's student. "Conditioned by our past to stay within our comfort zone, we allow our Inner Devil to defeat our voice of positivity and enthusiasm and end up beset by self-doubt. Captured in the Inner Devil's trap, we are now well set on the road to anxiety, ending in a lack of confidence. What does it take for us to overcome self-doubt?"

"Silencing our Inner Devil is rarely done. Haven't we often reflected on missed chances and wondered whether a different course of action might have been better? Or, wondered if our future would be brighter by following a different path that better suited our talents and passion? These are the times when the Inner Devil's mischief has succeeded, keeping us rooted, burdened by our past failures, unable to set out towards the bright future that we have visualised," concurred the Old Monk.

He continued, "There is only one way to defeat our Inner Devil at his game. The Inner Devil succeeds when he is invisible and when we are unaware of his destructive presence. When we stop to reflect on our fears and start questioning them, we engage in the simple and powerful act of self-reflection. That's when we begin to free ourselves from the machinations of our Inner Devil."

"Then our Inner Devil is no longer invisible." The Chief was smiling, as though struck by an epiphany.

"That is true. When we acknowledge that no new path was ever traversed free from obstacles, when we stop worrying about what others measure us to be, we begin to accept that each of us is a truly special individual. Knowing that our unique qualities shape us to be who we really are, we work at being truly ourselves. Then we are freed to move ahead."

It was clear that the Chief was noticeably more relaxed. In a casual tone, he asked his mentor, "Old Monk, in our conversations, you have usually referred to a literary or historical illustration that has helped me to cement my learning. Is there any anecdote that illustrates the predicament that I am facing now? One that might inspire me to reach the right decision."

"Yes, there's a historical story from over 2000 years ago that shares a similar predicament. I guess that the reference to Seneca the Younger has made me recall it, as it also happened at the time when the Roman Empire ruled the world. I will share it with you," stated the Old Monk.

"To begin, have you ever heard the expression, 'Crossing the Rubicon'?" When the Chief shook his head, he continued, "Crossing the Rubicon is often used as a metaphor that originates from a pivotal moment in Roman history, one that is steeped in high drama and with irreversible consequences.

The protagonist of this incident is Julius Caesar, possibly the most famous of all the Roman Emperors. The action started in 49 BCE, during the twilight of the Roman Republic, on the banks of the shallow Rubicon River, one of the many rivers that were scattered on the boundaries of the city of Rome. The Rubicon in northern Italy also marked the boundary between the Roman province of Cisalpine Gaul and the rest of the Roman Empire. While Gaul was governed by Caesar at that time, the huge Roman Empire was directly controlled by the Senate of Rome.

The story hinges on the important fact that it was strictly forbidden by Roman law for any General of Rome to cross this boundary with an army, as doing so was considered an act of treason and an open declaration of war against the Republic.

At the time, Caesar was a highly ambitious and controversial figure. He had gained immense power and popularity during his military campaigns in Gaul, but his rivals in the Roman Senate, particularly Pompey the Great, feared his growing influence. The Senate thus ordered Caesar to disband his army and return to

Rome as a private citizen, a demand that would strip him of his power and likely subject him to prosecution by his enemies.

It was a terrible ultimatum that was being offered to Julius Caesar. It is recounted that Caesar stood on the banks of the Rubicon, deliberating long and hard, torn between compliance and rebellion. Compliance would lead to the death of his ambition. He could defy the order and return to Gaul, where he faced the possibility of life in ignominy and exile, one that was not palatable for a person of his stature. While defying the Senate's order would lead to war and endanger the lives of his loyal troops.

According to historical accounts, he spent a long and restless night, deep in introspection. The next morning, declaring in Latin, *'Alea iacta est (The die is cast),'* he prepared to lead his troops across the river. It is also rumoured that he ordered the solitary bridge over the Rubicon to be burnt, symbolising that the path was irreversible. Caesar's act of defiance initiated a seven-year civil war that would ultimately lead to the end of the Roman Republic and the rise of the Roman Empire under his rule. Today, 'Crossing the Rubicon' serves as a powerful metaphor for making a fateful, irreversible decision, one that carries significant consequences and demands great courage in the face of uncertainty," concluded the Old Monk.

The Chief was mesmerised by the ancient tale and by the eloquence with which the Old Monk had masterfully recounted the story. The Old Monk had again used his conversational mastery to show the path. Applying the Old Monk's wisdom to his own life and career, he thought back to his hugely successful career trajectory and wondered if there had been other missed chances or exciting opportunities, that he had allowed to slip past. Would he be able to muster the courage now?

Lost in thought, the Chief gradually looked up. He noticed that the shadows from the bent tree had lengthened in the setting sun. A shadow from one of the branches was pointing outwards, seemingly beckoning to him. Was it sending, he wondered, sending a hidden message suggesting a path that he could take? He felt irresistibly drawn to look in that direction.

The horizon seemed to shimmer, like ripples running through a river. While accepting that it was probably his imagination playing tricks, he knew now that it was settled. The decision had been made. Like Julius Caesar of yore, once he had left the mountains and returned home, he felt ready to move ahead. Brimming with enthusiasm, the Chief now knew that he had crossed his Rubicon, ready to embrace an uncertain but exciting future.

A short while later, it was time to leave the bent tree. The bent tree would stand the test of time, standing resilient, its branches spreading wide beneath which so much wisdom had spread through to the Chief. Even if he were never to see the bent tree again, it was a connection between them that would last a lifetime.

They agreed to meet again the following day. As it was the last day of his vacation, the Chief asked the Old Monk if they could meet at the very spot where they had first met.

He had saved one last question for his mentor on what it meant to live a good life.

"In the time of your life, live—so that in that wondrous time you shall not add to the misery and sorrow of the world, but shall smile to the infinite delight and mystery of it."
– William Saroyan, The Time of Your Life

Chapter 12

The Inner Devil

THE INNER DEVIL

Some years ago, it wasn't that long ago,
A time when I, happy, went with the flow.
Confident, full of zest, I left my comfort zone,
Walked magical paths into the unknown.

Then I had found a path so perfect,
A shame it would be to have it wrecked,
For it portrayed a future that shone so brightly,
Lit up my path, a beacon on a dark night.

But as I brooded on the steps to take,
Worried that it's a blunder I'll make.
Burdens of my past weighed me down,
Won't what goes around come around?
Our past has much we don't speak about,
Scary recollections we can't boot out,
Yesteryear memories that flood our heads,
The doubts we have come to dread?

For, within my being, lurks an Inner Devil,
He's been the curse since medieval times.
Business for him is to mess with my head,
Root me to paths that the timid tread.

When my stocks crash and the funds dry,
That's when I find this devil close by.
Standing beside me in the games I lose,
Knows he's the cause of the path I chose.

Much as I try to keep him in rein,
He only submits if the stake's mundane.
But, when I find myself out of control,
You may be sure he's out on parole.

Finally, today, when I'm at my wits' end,
'Cause he's driven me around the bend,
I wonder how to disown him,
When he can appear, seemingly on a whim.

To banish the devil, don't catch his tail,
It'll fight for freedom, tooth and nail,
What's worse, there's often more than one.
They can't all be out-fought or out-run.

Chance is known to favour the brave,
The Inner Devil's a creature to enslave,
Any illusion of self-doubt you shake loose,
Be fearless, seek no refuge in an excuse.

The Devil works with a cloak of invisibility,
Unveiled reveals the Devil's vulnerability.
When you catch him out, then he's exposed,
And soon, he'll vanish to parts undisclosed.

Doubt draws on memory; treat it as trash,
Sort through the data, clear your cache,
Rebuild belief; it's a simple technique.
Paths open; you hit a winning streak.

<h1>Chapter 13</h1>

The Seeker

The taste of victory, when it arrives, isn't fleeting—it's something to savour, a slow burn that lingers and intensifies, becoming utterly addictive.

The tennis club is nestled amidst lush greenery. The afternoon sun is starting to mellow, casting a golden hue over the grass courts. In a shaded corner of the club's outdoor patio, two doubles partners sit side by side, enjoying a well-earned break after their hard-earned victory.

The younger partner is a woman, still in her tennis gear, her eyes sparkling with the energy of youth as she sits sipping on a tall glass of lemonade. Leaning back in her chair, legs stretched out, racquet lightly tapping the floor, one can't help but notice that while her face is still flushed from the exertions of the match, she wears a satisfied smile.

Beside her, sits the Chief, now a senior man in his late fifties, with silver hair and a salt-and-pepper beard, holding a glass of iced tea. His posture is more relaxed, shoulders slightly slumped in contented weariness. He's wearing a vintage-style white t-shirt, now marked with the faint signs of sweat, and his racquet leans against the table. There's a look of contentment on his face as if each point they won took him back to his younger days when tennis was not just a game but a passion.

They exchange a few words between sips, laughing over a particularly difficult game they managed to win. The young woman reminds him about his still quick reflexes, while he grins and waves it off, pretending it was just luck. A gentle breeze sweeps across the patio, cooling them down, as their conversation focuses on their shared love for the game and how they've blended as a team.

Around them, the hum of the club continues with the soft clatter of dishes and the murmur of other members chatting, but for now, they are content to share a comforting space in their own world—basking in the glow of achievement and savouring the moment.

The Chief notices how his partner gradually shifts the conversation to more introspective topics. He is no longer surprised to find this shift, for it has been happening in recent times in several conversations with his friends and colleagues. Though, he would admit that his tennis partner seemed to be a lot more curious than most. In fact, he had mentally begun to call her a 'Seeker'.

Seekers, in the Chief's vernacular, were those driven by curiosity to seek out life's deeper meaning. Thoughtful and reflective by nature, they value authenticity and desire meaningful connections with those who can offer perspective and guidance. In their journey of self-discovery, they aren't looking for easy answers, instead always striving to understand themselves and the world on a more fundamental level.

Her gaze fixed somewhere in the depths of her glass of lemonade, the Seeker slowly said, "A few days back on this same court where we played an hour ago, I played a singles match. I was coasting comfortably on my way to victory when inexplicably my game fell apart. Thereafter, I was unable to recoup and lost miserably.

It is a terrible feeling to lose when you know that you could have comfortably won."

She continued, "As I reflect on the circumstances, I am led to believe that the turning point happened when I missed an easy shot. It brought about a state of self-doubt about my quality of play. I began to question my shot selection and direction of play. Soon I was a bundle of nerves, though to the outside eye, I might have still looked to be in control. On the contrary, today I was able to play freely. I am left wondering what the difference was between the way I played then and today."

Listening to the Seeker describing her predicament, the Chief's mind drifted to a time when he had found himself in a similar state of dealing with self-doubt. The Old Monk, he recalled, had helped him manoeuvre past that challenge. In a soft tone, he said, "I have found that self-doubt has a way of creeping in unexpectedly, often at the most critical moments. All it took was your single missed shot to open the door to uncertainty, which in turn led to a loss of confidence; your every decision became clouded by hesitation. It is true that the challenge is less about overcoming opponents, but in mastering the inner battle within one's own mind."

"You presented my situation so well," the Seeker sounded relieved, though it didn't take but a moment for her to again say irritably. "I've mentioned it before, but my search for someone who can really guide me is still on. It is a pity that whenever I connect with someone who might be a guide or a coach, they tend to offer me all the 'answers'. Somehow, that never works out. I would rather find someone who helps me discover the answers myself. It's so hard to know where to start, or even know who to trust."

The Chief nodded and said, "I understand. You're looking for someone who listens deeply, allows you to take your time and doesn't impose their own truth. They nudge you towards finding your path, a truth that is your own. Humility and patience—those are the qualities you need to look for."

"That's so true," the Seeker sighs. "Those with whom I have spoken are ready to freely share their views and opinions, but all that they do is project their own experience onto mine, assuming that it would be identical to mine. That doesn't feel right. I want someone who helps me figure it out in my own way, not someone telling me what they think is best for me."

"That's a common trap. The right guide won't tell you what to do; they may share their own struggles, but they'll never assume yours are the same. They offer a gentle hand, not a firm push," said the Chief, capturing the Seeker's thoughts. "Whatever the result, win or lose, you are the only one playing the game. So, the right person will help you discover what you already know, what's inside you that will get you the best result."

The Seeker pauses, staring again into her glass, feeling the weight of her own frustration. Her thoughts swirl as she lets the Chief's words sink in. Was it so hard, she wonders, to find someone who truly set her on the path to self-discovery? A wave of doubt washes over her—what if she never finds this elusive guide?

Her eyes cloud over, and the vulnerability of admitting this feeling of uncertainty weighs on her. Could her endless search mean she's simply not ready to trust anyone? Or worse, not ready to trust herself? The effort of overcoming the overwhelming sound of outside voices seemed daunting.

The Chief leans forward slightly, his gaze steady, but he doesn't interrupt her. He knows the Seeker needs this space to deal with her own fears. The inner turmoil that the Seeker is going through is familiar to him for it wasn't that long ago; he could recall as if it was yesterday when he was grappling with the same inner battle.

After a long moment, the Seeker inhales deeply, blinking back the clouds of doubt. Her mind drifts, pondering her past connections, remembering the subtle disappointment she felt each time someone tried to lead her instead of walking beside her. The frustration tightens in her chest again.

The Seeker finally speaks, her voice quieter now, "Sometimes, I wonder if it's even possible to find such a guide. Maybe it's an unrealistic search. Is it that I am lazy, seeking help elsewhere rather than looking within? Maybe I'm asking for too much. What if the problem is to be fixed by me, not anyone else?"

When she continues, her voice is firmer. "I want someone who can help me overcome my uncertainty, who lets me be confused, and maybe even lets me fail a little, without stepping in to 'fix' things." She frowns, the thought lingering in the air as if she doesn't expect an answer.

"Can you recall a short while ago, we were on the brink of losing our match? You were about to receive our opponent's serve, and if your return had missed, it would cost us the game and the match. I could sense that you were very tense, anxious that you might let us down. What happened next?" The Chief leaned back now.

"Yes, I was a bundle of nerves at that stage," The Seeker continued speaking but with relief in her tone. "Then suddenly something happened. Suddenly, it was as though time stood still, I felt my anxiety melting away and I played a return shot that went smoothly past the other player for a winner."

She was silent for a while, reliving those moments. The Chief stayed relaxed, as though aware of the insight she was about to announce.

"Do you know," she continued, "I feel that it was your presence that changed my emotional state. Even in these tough situations, you didn't try to advise or pressurise me. All I sensed flowing from you was an unruffled calmness that immediately rubbed off on me and comforted me. That's who I've been craving to find, a guide who doesn't try to control my situation but helps me manage it as it unfolds. How do you find someone like that? People like that don't exactly advertise themselves."

"No, isn't it natural that they won't?" In a soft voice, the Chief added, "Sometimes, they're the quietest ones in the room, unnoticed until you really need them. They're like a still presence amidst the chaos. I once met someone like that—a mentor of sorts, though he wouldn't have called himself one."

"Who was that?" The Seeker was intrigued.

"Well, he never mentioned his name, so I started calling him the Old Monk. He never claimed to be a part of any formal religious order or said that he was any sort of a teacher, but he carried this quiet wisdom that comes through lifetimes of experience. He never drew attention to himself. You wouldn't notice him unless you were really looking." The Chief appeared pensive, distant. It was as though the Old Monk was back in his life.

"If they are so difficult to find, how did you meet him?" The Seeker's curiosity had reached a new high.

The Chief said cheerfully, "It would be easy to call it serendipitous or written into my destiny, for it was a long time ago when I first met the Old Monk while on vacation. Looking back, though, I am convinced that such meetings are pre-ordained, as though there is a higher power that pulls us towards a force like the Old Monk."

"I am sure that you would have come across many wise persons in your life. What made him unique, so different from the others?" asked the Seeker.

"Throughout my stay in the mountains, we had many meetings and deep conversations. I must admit that, initially, I was full of scepticism. Then gradually a sense of comfort crept into our conversations. It wasn't like any grand revelation, but I started to look forward to our conversations. His calmness rubbed off on me. It wasn't just what he said, but his demeanour. He had this sereneness about him as if he'd seen life's worst storms and come through unshaken. When I mentioned that the path I had chosen was drifting and there was a sense of feeling lost, he nudged me to look deeper within myself. He didn't offer quick fixes or draw detailed maps. Rather, he'd just be there, asking me to look within myself, a quiet reflection, helping me see the bigger picture without being too close to the problem."

"That," exclaimed the Seeker, "sounds like exactly who I've been looking for. Someone who helps you stay grounded when life feels like it's spinning out of control, while at the same time nudging me to fearlessly move ahead."

"Yes, that's exactly who he was. He wouldn't hand you answers on a silver platter. But when you were struggling, grappling to find the answer, maybe at your wit's end, he'd offer a small piece of wisdom, and it would stay with you, helping you find your way back to yourself." The Chief was speaking, reflecting carefully on his words. "He believed that the virtuous life is like a dance between karma and dharma—what we're dealt with and how we respond. And when you weren't sure how to move, he'd remind you that both were in your hands."

"Later, I learned that he called it the path of 'virtuous living'—the essence of one's purpose. Or, that which is simplistically known as 'Dharma' to others," the Chief continued.

The Seeker said softly, "I wonder if I've ever met anyone like that. Or maybe I just haven't been paying attention."

"Yes," said the Chief. "That is possible. People like the Old Monk don't force themselves into your life. They're there when you're ready, and sometimes you don't notice them until you need them most. They're always around, quietly watching, guiding, and never demanding attention."

"How will I know when he is around?" the Seeker seemed anxious.

"I am sure that the Old Monk will appear." The Chief was smiling. "Or maybe, he's already moving quietly in your life, waiting for you to recognise him. It's not about grand gestures or big moments. It's in the small moves, the subtle actions, the unobtrusive guidance. And when you do, you'll realise that his presence has been there all along, a quiet hand guiding you towards your own light. He will help you feel like you can breathe again, even when life feels overwhelming. And remind you, gently, that the path you're on is exactly where you need to be, even if it's full of uncertainties. When the time is right, you'll see."

Suddenly, the Seeker's face broke into a wide grin. "It's possible," she announced, "that I may have already found him. I think he's in front of me, just waiting to be acknowledged."

"That," said the Chief, reacting with an equally broad smile, "is entirely possible."

"In order to gain possession of ourselves, we have to have some confidence, some hope of victory. And in order to keep that hope alive, we must usually have some taste of victory. We must know what victory is and like it better than defeat."
– Thomas Merton

Chapter 14

Who is the Old Monk

The Old Monk moves silently among us,
Shares his wisdom freely, without fuss.
Available on call, yet noticed not at all,
Quite like the proverbial fly on the wall.
He is shaped from that unique mould.
Where you don't find him, young nor old,
Though with a demeanour so scholastic,
You might take him to be a monastic.
As the School of Hard Knocks grinds away,
When fate deals bad hands day by day
You search for the grit to take a stand,
The Old Monk's around to lend a hand.
When the ball's tossed into your court,
You worry that the return will fall short,
Leave all action to be met by your karma,
That's when Old Monk points to Dharma.
Life's journey can shine clear and bright,
If we have a mentor to help show the light.
A truth that is known to but a fortunate few,
Who find their Old Monk and break through.

Chapter 15

The Virtuous Life

What lies beyond the blue mountains?

The setting sun spread its shadows across the lawns of the tennis club. The Seeker was long gone, and only a few old-timers remained seated on the grounds, relaxing in an unspoken camaraderie. It was that time of day the Chief most enjoyed when he could let his mind roam freely. Today, probably due to his bringing it up with the Seeker, he recalled his conversation with the Old Monk on the last day of his vacation. It was then that the Old Monk spoke about what it meant to live the 'virtuous life', almost as though he knew that they might not meet again. The entirety of their conversation had remained rooted in the Chief's mind, for he recalled it often, as he was doing now.

He had started their conversation, in the usual manner, by asking a question on a topic that bothered him. "I often wonder," he began, "In a world that's always changing, and full of so much conflict, can someone really live a good life?"

When he put forth the question, it was in a tone of earnest curiosity. He had always sensed a deep-seated restlessness, an emotional tension, whenever he was grappling with the complexities of life and searching for guidance amidst uncertainty.

"That's a broad question," the Old Monk replied, smiling warmly. "Yes, it is a noble path that you wish to follow, but far from an easy one. Over the course of their lives, most people muddle through as though they are stuck in a kind of fog and unable to see ahead. They act without thinking, just going through the motions, unaware of any deeper purpose. Have you felt that way sometimes?"

"Yes, I do. I've been there," confessed the Chief. He spoke in a voice that had a mixture of resignation and a recognition of the weariness of the cycles of unconscious living. "Even now, despite all our conversations, there are moments when I react without really knowing why. Like I'm just going through life without thinking."

There was, he conceded, an uncomfortable vulnerability in his admission that he often felt lost in the 'fog' of life, just going through the motions.

"Exactly," the Old Monk said firmly. "Most of the time we're driven by our conditioning, many habits that have taken root and the influence of outside forces. The good news is that you're starting to be aware of this—well, that's the first step. The next step, I must caution, is a challenging one. It is a stage where you begin to want things, you're driven to succeed and to be recognised. A stage that is driven by burning ambition. Can you recognise this stage, too?"

As the Old Monk was gently guiding him through these reflections, the Chief recalled that his emotional state shifted from initial frustration to a smouldering passion, particularly when discussing ambition. As he connected with his inner drive for success, he felt awake, lit up with energy, but even through this excitement, there was palpably an undercurrent of dissatisfaction: "You know that it's the stage where I am right now—chasing goals, pushing myself. The problem is that even when I get what I want, it's never enough. It feels like I always need more and set myself another set of goals. It's frustrating." It was this duality—the burning desire to achieve, coupled with the awareness of its limitations—that infused his words with a sense of inner conflict.

Old Monk nodded knowingly, "Doubtless, ambition can be a great motivator, but one that is rooted in desire. That restlessness you speak about is because you're always seeking something new, looking for a sense of recognition outside yourself. Always wanting, but never fully satisfied. Why do you think that is?"

It was, the Chief remembered, a pivotal moment. When he expressed uncertainty about his pursuits, admitting that some of his goals "probably don't matter in the long run," he sensed that he was on the verge of a dawning realisation that perhaps what he had been chasing wasn't aligned with his deeper values. All it needed was a quieter, more introspective moment, the need to start peeling back the layers of his own psyche.

As the Old Monk went further, touching on the idea that his restlessness was tied to external recognition, the Chief's uncertainty became more pronounced. His earlier bravado waned and his voice grew more tentative as he agreed, "That is right, how do I break out of that cycle?"

"That's the tough part. To be able to start acting with understanding, not just reacting out of habit or confusion. When you stop being driven only by what you want and start focusing on what's beneficial for others—that's when the shift happens. You begin to find clarity and it is also where peace floods your being. That is what I call the 'virtuous life'," the Old Monk said in a clear tone.

"So, living a virtuous life means not chasing after things for myself, but doing what's right for everyone." he asked curiously. Though intrigued, the Chief wasn't entirely convinced; his tone was cautious, almost as if testing the waters of a new form of philosophy.

Old Monk replied, "Exactly. It's about acting from a place of clarity and wisdom, instead of chasing and being chased by your desires."

"The path to the virtuous life starts with being aware," he continued. "You must start paying attention to your experiences—what you see, what you feel. When you're fully present, you can start to see the world as it is, not just how you think it is or want it to be. Do you think you can start living that way?"

The Chief asked, "Is living just about noticing things?"

"Only partly true," the Old Monk was patient. "When you observe the world with an open mind, you start to see the truth more clearly.Yet it's not just about observation. You must also reflect on what you experience and think about it deeply. Have you tried doing that?"

"Honestly, not as much as I should," he said, a little sheepishly. "It's hard to make sense of things when I'm feeling all these different emotions. Then, I get trapped in my own head a lot."

"That's normal," the Old Monk reassured him. "The mind is always busy, full of emotions and thoughts. Awareness grows with practice. You can also seek wisdom from mentors, guides, or sacred texts—they offer guidance. Incidentally, how often do you seek help from others?"

"Hmm, not very often," the Chief admitted. "I usually try to figure things out on my own." There was a softness in his reply. It was difficult to accept that he rarely sought help from others, a concern that tackling his struggles in isolation might have brought about a quiet loneliness. As he continued to contemplate, he arrived at the uncomfortable realisation of how this tendency to rely on himself might have limited his growth.

"I agree that it is very good to trust in oneself," said the Old Monk in an encouraging note, sensing his discomfort. "There's value in that, but sometimes, we need the insights of others to help us see more clearly. Another way is by discernment. Confusion happens when we mistake what's temporary for what's eternal, or when we think something is pure when it's not. Haven't there been times when you found this happening?"

"I'm not sure… I guess sometimes I get caught up in things that probably don't matter in the long run," he said thoughtfully. "Like chasing after things that aren't really important."

"Exactly. When you focus on what aligns with your true self and let go of the rest, life becomes simpler. That's when you begin to live virtuously," the Old Monk said, smiling.

"So, is it about living in harmony with my inner self?" the Chief asked. He was still attempting to grasp the concept.

"Yes, when you detach from the constant pull of the material world, you can start to align with your inner self's deeper intent. It's like clearing a foggy mirror—you see yourself and the world more clearly," the Old Monk added. "Practices like meditation and self-reflection help with this."

"And is leading the virtuous life, the path to finding fulfilment?" asked the Chief, looking for reassurance.

"Fulfilment doesn't come from external achievements or material success," the Old Monk clarified. "It comes from cultivating inner awareness, living a balanced life, and continually staying on the path to finding wisdom. It is when you are totally aligned with your true self that you will act with clarity and compassion. The limitations of the material world will have less of a pull on you. Do you think you're ready for that shift?"

"It sounds like it's a long and arduous journey, but yes, I want to start," the Chief said resolutely, for he found that his initial resistance had slowly shifted to eagerness.

His initial scepticism—"Is it just about noticing things?"—was now a more earnest desire to learn. Then, when he suddenly asked, "How do I start?" he sensed the shift, the movement from being filled with doubt towards a yearning for transformation.

His emotional state had evolved into one of resolution and purpose. Looking back, once he declared the desire to start on the long and arduous journey, there was a sense of determination, a readiness to embark on the path to virtuous living. The initial uncertainty had transformed into a commitment to growth, even if the road ahead seemed challenging.

"The brightest part of this journey," encouraged the Old Monk, "is that it is more than about freeing yourself. As you move along the path, growing in clarity and wisdom, your actions will naturally begin to uplift others. A virtuous life radiates outward—it benefits the people around you and the world around you. Can you imagine the joy that you will radiate?'

"Yeah, I think I do," exclaimed the Chief. "It's like by changing myself, I can help create more harmony around me, right?"

"'Exactly," the Old Monk now had a warm smile. "You become a force for balance, compassion, and truth. The path that you now see is through the eyes of your inner self. It is when you live in harmony with your inner self that you begin to live in harmony with the greater whole. You are then on the path to virtuous living."

These parting words by the Old Monk, for it was their last conversation, had struck a deep chord in the Chief. He felt as though a burden he had been carrying was lifted; it was replaced by a sense of purpose and connection to something greater than himself. Thereafter, he often reminded himself that his journey was not only for his personal fulfilment but for the betterment of those around him, contributing to a larger harmonious whole.

The sun had finally dipped below the horizon, but its fading light still lingered, casting a golden glow across the rugged mountains. The sky, once a deep blue, was now awash with warm hues, as though the heavens themselves were touched by gold. The jagged peaks stood in silhouette; their sharp edges softened by the amber light that draped over them like a delicate veil. The air was still, the world quiet, save for the faint rustle of leaves in the evening breeze.

The Chief sat motionless, his sharp eyes drawn to an eagle soaring effortlessly through the vast sky. The bird circled with grace; its wide wings catching the last of the sun's rays, glowing almost ethereal in the dimming light. The eagle moved closer for a moment, its path curving towards him as if in silent communication, before swooping away again. Its flight was steady and purposeful, and in that moment, the Chief felt an inexplicable connection, as though the eagle were calling to him. It was as if the bird beckoned him, whispering through its flight, "Let's meet on the mountaintop."

He blinked, shaking his head slightly, brushing away the notion as nothing more than a fleeting fancy, his imagination running wild in the tranquillity of the evening. And yet, the idea lingered, curling itself around his thoughts. The memory of the Old Monk surfaced, unbidden but not unwelcome. The thought of meeting him again—of perhaps seeking his wisdom on those very mountains—was irresistible.

There was a deep stirring within him. It had been a long time since he had ventured to the peaks, where the wind felt crisper, and the silence more profound. Maybe the eagle's call wasn't a mere figment after all. Perhaps, a visit to the mountains was long overdue.

Chapter 16

The Eagle in My Soul

The eagle in my soul, I know him not.
One might well ask if he is my blind spot,
A restless invader that asks more from me,
While I rest content to stay low-key.

An eagle's hidden in my soul, knows me well,
It's my fears, I sense that it wants to dispel.
When I feel its presence, albeit fleetingly
I am encouraged to start tasks daringly.

The eagle in my soul wants to be free,
When it soars, then I foresee my goals,
Astride its wings, there's an endless view,
Helping me choose the right path to pursue.

The eagle commands my soul, is no longer silent,
I absorbed its presence and am now content,
Like a stiletto piercing my soul, a traceless knife,
It frees my spirit, springing it to life.

Epilogue

O ld Monks don't only reside in the mountains.
It is in human nature to be dissatisfied with our present lot. We keep ourselves perennially busy exploring, and grabbing territory, yet never satisfied and wanting for more. In this quest, we continually seek those who can help us reach a usually elusive destination.

> In mankind lies the urge to explore,
> That keeps us seeking distant shores.
> We watch the astronaut free the skies,
> While the sailor cuts the ocean to size.
>
> Moving outside our comfort zone,
> Navigating the path to the unknown.
> Our voyages are a quest for learning,
> Often returning none the wiser, still yearning.

Traversing the pages of this book, on your journey with the Chief, you, the Reader, will have noticed that in every conversation the Old Monk never ever shows the path. Rather, he nudges the Chief to find the direction best suited to reach the destination.

Hark, one needn't travel anywhere,
A true explorer's journey starts nowhere.
What's the use of travelling miles, to sink or swim,
When all of discovery lies within.

If we are alert to their presence, Old Monks are everywhere donning the garbs of mentors, teachers, coaches, or guides.

Are you ready to seek out an Old Monk—or even better—be one?

Acknowledgements

With Old Monks for parents—this book is dedicated to them—that's when the mind opens, alert to seeking and finding Old Monks everywhere.

So, my gratitude to the many Old Monks who helped shape my life, notably Timothy Gallwey, John O'Neil, Sir John Whitmore, Professor Mihaly Csikzentmihalyi, Captain Pavan Murthy, Professor Thirunarayana, all legends in the worlds of business, sports, academia, with whom every interaction, every conversation was an opportunity for deep introspection and learning.

A huge shout-out to my family. To Nimu, my wonderful better half, without whose constant encouragement and nudging this book wouldn't have happened. To Nitin, my son, whose insights helped develop the core theme of the narrative, and Uttara, my daughter, for absorbing the poems and creating the Old Monk website. For Emily and Govind, the lovely additions to our family.

I am super grateful to my extended family of brothers, sisters, nieces and nephews. It's our bonding that keeps my creative energy flowing.

A big thanks to my editor, Jaya Mirra, and the team at Notion Press for their support.

The Old Monk poems were first written and shared with my batchmates at the Indian Institute of Technology, Madras, who egged me on, and I kept them flowing. Thanks, fellows!

Finally, I remain indebted to every Old Monk who nourished my path.

About the Author

Krishna Kumar Marayil, based in Bengaluru, India, is the Founder and Master Coach of the Intrad School of Executive Coaching. A pioneer in Leadership Coaching in India, Krishna Kumar's journey of over four decades reflects his deep commitment to lifelong learning and growth. Over the years, he has taken on diverse roles as a senior corporate executive, entrepreneur, professional tennis coach, B-school professor, independent Board member, and Executive Coach, all of which have shaped his unique perspective on leadership and human potential.

In Crossing the Rubicon, Krishna Kumar blends his insights and experiences into a profound exploration of self-discovery and transformation. His own journey with the Old Monk, much like the Chief's, is far from over, promising new paths to be walked and deeper lessons to be uncovered.

The author can be reached at
krishna.kumar@thewisdomofoldmonk.com